POLARITY THERAPY

A Comprehensive Guide To Understanding, Applying, And Elevating Your Well-Being With Polarity Therapy

WILFREDO CARSON

INTRODUCTION

Polarity Therapy, an alternative therapeutic method, takes a comprehensive approach to health and wellness. This technique, founded on ancient knowledge and modern science, seeks to balance and harmonize the body's energy flow to enhance physical, mental, and emotional well-being. In this examination, we will look at the fundamental components of Polarity Therapy, including its welcome and purpose, historical antecedents, and the concepts that underpin this intriguing approach to well-being.

Welcome and Purpose of the Book

At the heart of any comprehensive examination of Polarity Therapy is a knowledge of its welcome and purpose.

The goal of Polarity Therapy is to promote a balanced flow of life force, or prana, throughout the body. This book helps readers understand Polarity Therapy's philosophy, methodologies, and applications. The goal is to provide anyone, whether practitioners or curious enthusiasts, with information that encourages a greater appreciation for the interconnectivity of energy, mind, and body. As we embark on this journey, we are warmly welcomed to embrace a holistic approach to health and healing.

A Brief History of Polarity Therapy

To understand the evolution of Polarity Therapy, we must first go back to its historical beginnings. Polarity Therapy, created by Dr. Randolph Stone, a chiropractor, naturopath, and osteopath, originated in the early twentieth century as a result of Stone's thorough research into many therapeutic systems. Inspired by Ayurveda, Traditional Chinese Medicine, and Western holistic approaches, Stone created a one-of-a-kind system that focuses on the dynamic interaction of energy in the human body. Polarity Therapy's historical narrative therefore connects the threads of various healing traditions, resulting in a tapestry that demonstrates a deep understanding of the universal laws controlling health and vitality.

An Overview of Polarity Therapy Principles

The ideas that underpin Polarity Therapy provide a comprehensive framework for understanding the dynamics of energy flow inside the body. Polarity Therapy claims that abnormalities in the body's energy field cause physical, mental, and emotional imbalances. Polarity Therapy seeks to restore and sustain optimal health by treating these disturbances and facilitating a balanced flow of energy. The three major principles—energy currents, elements, and energy centers—guide practitioners across the intricate terrain of the body's energetic architecture.

Energy Currents

Polarity Therapy revolves around the concept of energy currents, which symbolize the dynamic movement of life energy within the body. These currents, which are classified as positive, negative, and neutral, reflect the polarity present in nature. Positive energy corresponds to expansive and activating powers, whilst negative energy represents contracting and consolidating forces. The neutral energy acts as a balancing factor, regulating the interaction of positive and negative forces. Polarity Therapy uses a variety of treatment procedures to balance and maximize these energy currents, encouraging an equilibrium that promotes the body's natural healing abilities.

Elements

In Polarity Therapy, the five elements—earth, water, fire, air, and ether—are archetypal metaphors for various qualities and components of life energy. Each element is associated with distinct traits and corresponds to various areas of the body. Earth, for example, is associated with solidity and grounding, and it is frequently linked to the lower body. Water signifies flexibility and adaptability, which resonates with the pelvic region. Fire represents transformation and life, and it corresponds to the abdomen area.

Air is related to movement and communication, as it corresponds to the chest and respiratory system. Finally, ether represents the subtle and spiritual aspects, linking to the head and higher energy centers. Understanding and harmonizing these elemental energies is an essential component of Polarity Therapy methods.

<u>Energy Centers</u>

Polarity Therapy relies heavily on the human body's intricate network of energy centers, or chakras. These energy centers are aligned along the body's central axis and serve as focal areas for the reception, assimilation, and distribution of life force. Each chakra is associated with a distinct physiological, psychological, and spiritual function. For example, the root chakra, located at the base of the spine, is linked to survival and grounding, whereas the crown chakra, located at the top of the head, is associated with spiritual connection and higher awareness. Polarity Therapy uses a variety of treatments, including massage and energy balancing, to maintain the proper functioning and alignment of these energy centers, allowing for a harmonic flow of energy throughout the body.

Application of Polarity Therapy

After exploring the fundamental principles of Polarity Therapy, it is critical to investigate its practical applications. Polarity Therapy provides a diverse set of therapeutic modalities, including bodywork, diet, exercise, and self-awareness practices.

The confluence of various methods attempts to correct energy field imbalances, improving overall healing and well-being. Bodywork, a key component of Polarity Therapy, entails gentle touch, manipulation, and energy balancing to relieve tension and promote the free flow of energy. Dietary recommendations are consistent with the fundamental principles, emphasizing the consumption of foods that balance and support certain energy properties. Exercise programs suited to individual demands improve overall vitality and energy flow. Furthermore, self-awareness techniques such as meditation and breathwork help people grow mindfulness and connect with the body's natural wisdom.

In conclusion, Polarity Therapy is a comprehensive approach to wellness that combines ancient wisdom with modern understanding.

We learn about a system that sees the body as an intricate web of energy currents, elements, and centers by delving into its welcome and purpose, historical roots, and core concepts. Polarity Therapy provides a road map for both practitioners and enthusiasts to navigate the landscape of holistic well-being, treating imbalances in the body's energy field using a comprehensive approach. As we go deeper into the complexities of Polarity Therapy, we uncover a profound philosophy that challenges us to accept the interdependence of energy, mind, and body, fostering a path to optimal health and vitality.

CHAPTER 1
FOUNDATIONS OF POLARITY THERAPY

Polarity Therapy, created by Dr. Randolph Stone in the mid-twentieth century, is a comprehensive approach to health and well-being that combines concepts from Eastern and Western healing traditions.

Polarity Therapy's fundamental premise is that the body's energy flows in certain patterns and that balancing these energy flows promotes optimal health. This therapy is inspired by several ancient systems, including Ayurveda, Traditional Chinese Medicine, and Western scientific ideas. One of the core tenets of Polarity Therapy is the recognition that the body is more than simply a physical thing; it is a complex interaction of energy fields.

By detecting and harmonizing these energy systems, practitioners hope to aid the body's natural healing processes.

<u>Understanding energy in polarity therapy:</u>

Polarity Therapy is based on a knowledge of energy and its dynamic character in the human body. Polarity Therapy views energy as a physical force that runs through the body in distinct patterns rather than a theoretical construct.

This energy is said to take three major forms: positive, negative, and neutral. The positive pole represents the stimulating and activating element of energy, whilst the negative pole represents relaxation and receptivity.

The neutral pole acts as a balancing factor, promoting a peaceful exchange of positive and negative energy.

Polarity Therapy practitioners emphasize the importance of free-flowing energy in promoting health and preventing sickness. Blockages or imbalances in energy flow are regarded to be antecedents to physical and emotional disorders, hence restoring balanced energy is a primary goal of therapeutic intervention.

The Five Elements of Polarity Therapy:

Polarity Therapy embraces the ancient notion of the Five Elements, which is central to many Eastern philosophies and healing practices. These elements—Earth, Water, Fire, Air, and Ether—represent distinct traits and energy that interact throughout the body.

Each element is associated with a certain organ, emotion, or physiological function. Polarity Therapy uses the Five Elements as a framework to study the many expressions of energy within the body-mind complex.

For example, Earth represents stability and foundation, Water fluidity and adaptation, Fire transformation and energy, Air movement and communication, and Ether the ethereal essence that transcends the material reality. Polarity Therapy practitioners seek to discover areas of imbalance and support the restoration of a harmonious energy flow in individuals by examining the balance and interplay of these aspects.

<u>Chakras and their significance:</u>

Polarity Therapy includes an investigation of the chakra system, which is based on ancient

Indian traditions, particularly yogic and Ayurvedic frameworks.

Chakras are energy centers located along the spine, each with its own set of physical, emotional, and spiritual characteristics. Polarity Therapy defines seven primary chakras, each of which corresponds to a different part of the body and plays an important role in an individual's overall health.

Mujaddara is the root chakra, Svadhisthana is the sacral chakra, Manipura is the solar plexus, Anahata is the heart chakra, Vishuddha is the throat chakra, Ajna is the third eye chakra, and Sahasrara is the crown chakra.

The health of these chakras is said to influence the corresponding organs and parts of the body, as well as the emotional and mental states.

Polarity Therapy practitioners use hands-on techniques, energetic exercises, and mindfulness practices to balance and align the chakras, promoting overall healing and optimal energy flow throughout the body.

Finally, Polarity Therapy represents a comprehensive and integrative approach to health and well-being, building on a rich tapestry of ancient wisdom and current thinking. The basis of this therapy is the understanding of the body's unique energy patterns, with a focus on balancing and harmonizing these energies for optimal health. The addition of the Five Elements and examination of the chakra system strengthen Polarity Therapy's holistic approach, giving a comprehensive framework for comprehending the dynamic interaction of energy within the human body-mind complex. Polarity Therapy, as a holistic treatment method, is always evolving, providing a unique viewpoint on health that transcends conventional boundaries and acknowledges the interdependence of physical, mental, and spiritual well-being.

CHAPTER 2
PRINCIPLES OF POLARITY THERAPY

Polarity Therapy is a holistic therapeutic approach that incorporates the idea of energy balance inside the human body. This therapeutic system is based on three main principles: neutral, positive, and negative. The neutral principle serves as the basic basis, signifying a condition of balance and equilibrium in the body's energy. This neutral condition is essential for maintaining good health and well-being. Polarity Therapy contends that interruptions in this neutral energy balance can result in a variety of bodily and mental disorders.

The other two principles, Positive and Negative, are opposites at opposite ends of the spectrum. Positive energy is distinguished by an expansive, outward flow, which is connected with attributes such as warmth, stimulation, and activity. In contrast, negative energy is characterized by a contractive, inward flow, which manifests as traits such as coldness, relaxation, and receptivity. The interaction of these polarities is thought to be necessary for the body's dynamic balance. Polarity Therapy practitioners think that understanding and using these concepts can help to restore balance and harmony, which promotes general health.

<u>Balancing energy flows:</u>

Polarity Therapy is based on the concept of balancing energy flows, which involves manipulating and harmonizing the body's energy currents. Practitioners use a variety of techniques to balance these energy flows, remove blockages, and promote the free passage of energy throughout the body. Bodywork is a core strategy in Polarity Therapy that involves practitioners applying gentle touch and manipulation to specific energy spots known as energy centers or zones. By targeting these spots, the therapist hopes to realign and regulate the flow of energy, improving overall well-being and vitality.

The body is viewed as a complicated network of energy pathways, with disturbances causing physical discomfort and mental suffering. Polarity Therapy acknowledges the interdependence of the body, mind, and spirit, emphasizing the need to correct energy imbalances at all levels. In addition to hands-on approaches, practitioners may use exercises, dietary recommendations, and lifestyle changes to help balance energy flows. This holistic approach recognizes that imbalances in one part of life can affect the entire energy system, necessitating a thorough and integrated approach to healing.

Polarity Therapy and Nervous System:

Polarity Therapy's deep link with the neurological system emphasizes its therapeutic impact on both physical and emotional well-being. The nervous system, which consists of both central and peripheral components, is responsible for delivering and directing impulses throughout the body. Polarity Therapy recognizes the impact of energy imbalances on the nervous system and works to correct these imbalances to restore normal functioning.

Polarity Therapy's Neutral, Positive, and Negative principles are strongly related to the autonomic nervous system (ANS).

The autonomic nervous system regulates involuntary body activities such as heart rate, digestion, and breathing rate. The Neutral principle is consistent with the ANS's balanced state, in which the sympathetic (fight or flight) and parasympathetic (rest and digest) branches are in equilibrium. Positive energy corresponds to the sympathetic nervous system, which is activated and stimulated, and negative energy refers to the parasympathetic nervous system, which is calming and relaxing.

Polarity Therapy strategies attempt to control the activity of the autonomic nervous system by encouraging a change from sympathetic dominance to parasympathetic balance.

This change is critical for stress reduction, relaxation, and the body's natural healing mechanisms. Polarity Therapy's hands-on therapies, breathwork, and energy exercises all help to modulate this process, allowing the energy principles and nervous system to work together harmoniously.

Furthermore, Polarity Therapy acknowledges the importance of the neurological system in the mind-body relationship. Emotional and mental well-being are inextricably linked to the functioning of the neurological system, and energy imbalances can cause psychological anguish. Polarity Therapy seeks to improve mental health by addressing energy fluxes and encouraging equilibrium, thus reducing anxiety, improving mood, and increasing general emotional resilience.

Finally, the concepts of Polarity Therapy include Neutral, Positive, and Negative energies, each of which is critical to sustaining dynamic homeostasis inside the body. Balancing energy flows using hands-on techniques and holistic approaches is essential to this treatment modality, which aims to address disruptions and improve general well-being. The complicated relationship between Polarity Therapy and the neurological system underlines the approach's potential to improve both physical and mental health, emphasizing the necessity of restoring balance throughout the body-mind-spirit continuum.

CHAPTER 3
TECHNIQUES OF POLARITY THERAPY

Bodywork and Polarity Therapy:

Bodywork is an essential component of Polarity Therapy, a comprehensive technique that seeks to balance and harmonize the flow of energy throughout the body. Polarity Therapy involves the practitioner using a variety of hands-on techniques to relieve energy blockages and improve the individual's vitality. This type of bodywork is founded on the idea that the human body is a dynamic energy system with many energetic patterns flowing through it. The practitioner uses gentle touch, manipulation, and palpation to detect and treat areas of tension or imbalance in the energy field.

One of the fundamental foundations of Polarity Therapy's bodywork is the understanding of three major energy forces: positive, negative, and neutral. These forces are related to specific parts of the body, and the practitioner strives to balance them so that energy can flow freely. The therapist uses skillful touch and manipulation to induce tension release, promote relaxation, and allow the vital life force to circulate more freely. Bodywork sessions may include a variety of techniques like rocking, cradling, and holding specific spots on the body, all to restore balance to the energetic system.

Additionally, bodywork in Polarity Therapy frequently focuses on the chakras, which are energy centers along the spine. To stimulate or relax these energy centers and promote balance, the practitioner may utilize specific hand positions and movements.

This holistic approach to bodywork goes beyond alleviating physical discomfort; it tries to harmonize an individual's physical, mental, and emotional elements, understanding their interdependence within the larger energy system.

Finally, massage in Polarity Therapy promotes balance and harmony within the energetic structure of the human body. Practitioners use expert touch and manipulation to relieve energy blockages, promote relaxation, and improve the individual's overall well-being.

Stretching and Movement Exercises:

Stretching and movement exercises are essential components of Polarity Therapy, helping to promote energy flow and equilibrium within the body.

Recognizing that stagnant energy can cause physical discomfort and mental suffering, Polarity Therapy integrates specialized exercises to stretch and mobilize the body. These exercises are designed to increase flexibility, relieve tension, and promote the smooth circulation of vital life force energy.

Stretching, in the context of Polarity Therapy, is more than just a physical practice; it is a way to connect with the body's energy aspects. Stretches are typically done mindfully and intentionally, with the participant encouraged to concentrate on the feelings and energy flow connected with each action. Polarity Therapy aims to improve the mind-body connection and maximize the advantages of stretching by introducing mindfulness into the process.

Polarity Therapy's movement exercises are intended to complement the stretching component by integrating dynamic and rhythmic patterns to enhance energy flow. These exercises may be influenced by other movement traditions, such as Qigong or Tai Chi, which emphasize fluidity and intentionality in each motion. Practitioners lead people through movement sequences that involve various muscle groups, joints, and energy pathways, encouraging vitality and balance.

Breath awareness is also an important component of Polarity Therapy's stretching and movement exercises. Conscious breathing is coordinated with each stretch or action, easing tension and creating calm.

The emphasis on the breath integrates the individual's physiological, energetic, and mental aspects, promoting a holistic approach to well-being.

To summarize, Polarity Therapy's stretching and movement activities go beyond the traditional definition of physical activity.

They are a focused and intentional activity that promotes the free flow of energy, increases flexibility, and fosters a harmonious connection between the body's energetic dimensions.

<u>Polarity Yoga and asanas:</u>

Polarity Yoga and Asanas are a subset of Polarity Therapy that uses yogic principles and postures to harmonize and balance the flow of energy throughout the body.

Yoga is viewed in Polarity Therapy as a holistic practice that blends breath, movement, and consciousness to promote energetic alignment rather than mere physical exercise. Polarity Yoga is a practice that combines precise asanas (postures), pranayama (breath control), and meditation techniques to accommodate each individual's unique energetic needs.

Polarity Yoga is founded on an understanding of the three major energy forces - positive, negative, and neutral - and how they emerge within the body. Asanas are chosen and sequenced to target specific energy centers and promote the free flow of vital life force.

The practitioner consciously explores each pose, focusing on the feelings, breath, and energy flow involved with the practice.

One distinguishing feature of Polarity Yoga is the use of energetic touch and alignment modifications by the therapist or instructor. This tailored instruction is intended to improve the individual's experience with each asana, guaranteeing appropriate alignment and optimal energy flow. The combination of yogic postures with Polarity Therapy concepts results in a distinct blend that goes beyond traditional yoga practices, providing a comprehensive approach to well-being.

Polarity Yoga sessions may also involve components of energy balancing and cleansing, in which the practitioner uses specialized techniques to remove energy blockages or disturbances in the body. Polarity Yoga is distinguished from traditional yoga practices by its integrative approach, which emphasizes the connectivity of the physical, energy, and mental elements. Polarity Yoga and Asanas are a specialized application of yogic concepts within the context of Polarity Therapy.

This practice, which combines particular postures, breath control, and energetic awareness, attempts to equalize the flow of energy, establish balance, and support the individual's general health. The incorporation of Polarity Therapy concepts adds a new level to the conventional practice of yoga, emphasizing the interaction of the body's energy forces with the ancient wisdom of yogic philosophy.

CHAPTER 4
ENERGY CENTERS, CHAKRAS, AND ZONES

Polarity Therapy is a holistic approach to health and wellness that includes the concept of energy centers, sometimes known as chakras. These energy centers are essential to the practice, reflecting an ancient understanding of the body's subtle energy system. In Polarity Therapy, the chakras are viewed as dynamic, interconnected centers of life force energy that influence physical, emotional, and mental health. The seven primary chakras, which run along the spine, connect to certain parts of the body and are regarded to play an important role in maintaining balance and harmony.

An in-depth examination of each chakra is necessary to comprehend Polarity Therapy. The first chakra, known as Muladhara or the Root Chakra, is located at the base of the spine and is related to grounding, stability, and basic survival instincts. Moving forward, the Sacral Chakra (Svadhisthana) is associated with creativity, sexuality, and emotions. The Solar Plexus Chakra (Manipura), located in the abdomen area, regulates personal power, self-esteem, and confidence. The Heart Chakra (Anahata) is located in the heart of the chest and represents love, compassion, and interpersonal interactions. The Throat Chakra (Vishuddha) governs speech and self-expression, whereas the Third Eye Chakra

(Ajna), located between the brows, is related to intuition and spiritual awareness.

Finally, the Crown Chakra (Sahasrara) on top of the head connects people to higher consciousness and the divine.

Each chakra has a distinct vibrational frequency that corresponds to various organs, glands, and body functions. In Polarity Therapy, balancing these energy centers is thought to be crucial for overall well-being. Practitioners use a variety of procedures to harmonize and align the chakras, to restore the body's natural flow of energy.

Understanding energy zones in the body is another critical component of Polarity Therapy. The term "energy zones" refers to certain regions where energy manifests or accumulates, which are linked to the chakra system.

Polarity Therapy classifies the body into three major zones: the head, chest, and pelvis. Each zone correlates to a unique physiological and psychological function, and practitioners aim to balance energy flow within these zones to improve overall vitality.

The head zone, for example, is linked to cerebral functions, sensory awareness, and increased consciousness. Polarity Therapy emphasizes the need to harmonize energy in this zone to reduce stress, improve mental clarity, and improve cognitive capabilities. Craniosacral treatment and energy balancing are used to correct imbalances in the head zone, encouraging relaxation and mental well-being.

The chest zone, which includes the heart and respiratory system, represents emotions, love, and connection. Polarity Therapy emphasizes the importance of balancing energy in this zone to promote emotional well-being and healthy relationships. Practitioners use massage and breathwork techniques to relieve tension and create a healthy flow of energy in the chest zone, which supports emotional balance and heart-centered life.

The pelvic zone, which includes the lower abdominal and reproductive organs, is linked to creativity, sexuality, and vital energy.

In Polarity Therapy, harmonizing the energy in this zone is regarded as critical for general vitality and well-being. Pelvic floor exercises and bodywork are used to resolve imbalances in the pelvis zone, enabling healthy creative expression and facilitating the passage of life force energy throughout the body.

Polarity Therapy's use of chakras and energy zones provides a complete framework for analyzing and treating imbalances in the body's subtle energy system. Recognizing the interconnection of various energy centers and zones allows practitioners to adjust their approach to fit the specific needs of each individual, promoting holistic well-being on physical, emotional, and spiritual levels. Polarity Therapy stands out as a comprehensive therapy that strives to reconcile the dynamic interaction of energies inside the human body, thanks to its intricate understanding of energy centers and zones.

CHAPTER 5
POLARITY THERAPY AND HEALTH

Polarity Therapy is a comprehensive approach to health and well-being created by Dr. Randolph Stone in the mid-twentieth century. This therapy is based on the idea that life energy, also known as chi or prana, flows through the body in distinct patterns.

The proper flow of this energy is essential for maintaining good health, and any disruptions or imbalances can cause physical, mental, or emotional problems. Polarity Therapy seeks to restore and balance the flow of energy throughout the body, promoting general health.

Applications for Mental Health:

One important feature of Polarity Therapy is its use in mental health. This technique is based on the premise that energy flow abnormalities might contribute to mental health issues. Polarity Therapy practitioners think that removing energy blockages and restoring balance can help ease symptoms linked with disorders including anxiety, sadness, and stress. Polarity Therapy-based mental health therapies frequently include bodywork, energy exercises, and counseling. Polarity Therapy tries to improve mental well-being by focusing on energy channels and acknowledging the mind-body interdependence.

Polarity Therapy for Physical Wellbeing:

Polarity Therapy is based on the idea that the body's energy field affects its overall health.

This therapy uses a variety of procedures to regulate and unblock the energy flow, which aids in physical recovery. Bodywork, which involves gentle manipulation of the body's energy centers and pathways, is an essential component of Polarity Therapy for physical well-being. Practitioners think that relieving tension, stagnation, or blockages in the energy flow allows the body to repair itself more effectively. Polarity Therapy may also include dietary recommendations and lifestyle changes to help the body heal naturally. Polarity Therapy's holistic approach recognizes the importance of physical, mental, and emotional factors in preserving total health.

Emotional Healing using Polarity Therapy:

Polarity Therapy also emphasizes emotional well-being and acknowledges the link of emotions to the body's energy system. Polarity Therapy involves identifying and correcting energetic imbalances that might develop as emotional problems. Practitioners employ a variety of practices, such as massage, breathwork, and energy exercises, to relieve emotional stress and produce a more balanced flow of energy. Polarity Therapy tries to improve emotional well-being by restoring energy balance. Polarity Therapy's holistic and integrative approach to emotional healing offers a unique viewpoint on the complex interplay between emotions and the body's energy system.

To summarize, Polarity Therapy provides a holistic approach to health by addressing the interdependence of the body, mind, and emotions. Its applications in mental health, bodily well-being, and emotional healing demonstrate the breadth of this holistic therapy. Polarity Therapy uses techniques such as massage, energy exercises, and lifestyle changes to restore balance to the body's energy system, encouraging general well-being.

The incorporation of these concepts into Polarity Therapy demonstrates a comprehensive knowledge of health that goes beyond standard techniques, making it a valuable modality in the field of complementary and alternative medicine.

CHAPTER 6
INTEGRATING POLARITY THERAPY WITH OTHER MODALITIES

Polarity Therapy is a comprehensive approach to health that uses a variety of treatments to balance the body's energies and improve general well-being. One important feature of this therapy method is combining Polarity Therapy with other modalities to increase its effectiveness and address a broader range of health conditions. Complementary therapies play an important role in this integration because they allow practitioners to mix multiple methods that work together to provide a more complete healing experience.

Complementary therapies, when used with Polarity Therapy, seek to improve therapeutic outcomes by targeting specific areas of an individual's health and encouraging synergistic effects. Acupuncture, massage therapy, herbal medicine, and energy healing modalities are some of the possible remedies. Acupuncture integration, for example, can assist activate certain energy meridians, which aligns with Polarity Therapy's concepts of restoring energy flow and balance in the body. Massage therapy, on the other hand, supports Polarity Therapy by encouraging relaxation, reducing tension, and facilitating energy flow throughout the body.

Herbal medicine can be used to supplement the body's natural healing processes, offering nutritional and energetic support while enhancing the advantages of Polarity Therapy.

Holistic Approaches to Wellness: Polarity Therapy is fundamentally a holistic approach that takes into account an individual's physical, mental, emotional, and energetic dimensions. When combined with other methods that follow a holistic concept, it forms a more comprehensive framework for improving wellness.

Holistic approaches, such as mindfulness, meditation, and yoga, are perfectly aligned with Polarity Therapy concepts. Mindfulness activities increase awareness of energy imbalances, whereas meditation promotes mental clarity and emotional equilibrium. Yoga, which focuses on breath and body movements, enhances Polarity Therapy by increasing flexibility, circulation, and energy flow. The combination of these holistic activities results in a symbiotic relationship that helps people achieve a deeper feeling of well-being.

Collaborative Practices: Collaborative practices entail the integration of various treatment modalities through a concerted effort by practitioners. Polarity Therapy may involve collaboration among practitioners from many professions such as acupuncture, chiropractic care, psychology, and nutrition.

A Polarity Therapy practitioner and a chiropractor, for example, can work together to address both energy imbalances and structural misalignments, resulting in a more holistic approach to healing. Integrating Polarity Therapy with Psychotherapy allows for a more comprehensive examination of mental and emotional well-being, recognizing the relationship between energy patterns and psychological states.

Nutritionists working with Polarity Therapy practitioners can create tailored dietary regimens that address the energetic demands discovered during Polarity Therapy sessions, thereby enhancing the overall therapeutic effect.

Finally, combining Polarity Therapy with other modalities increases its efficacy and broadens its reach in enhancing overall well-being. Complementary therapies provide a variety of tools and approaches that complement Polarity Therapy's concepts, resulting in a more nuanced and individualized approach to individual health.

Holistic approaches, which emphasize interrelated aspects of well-being, help to provide a more complete knowledge and application of Polarity Therapy. Collaborative techniques with professionals from several professions provide a holistic approach that addresses all aspects of an individual's health. The incorporation of these ideas not only improves the practice of Polarity Therapy but also highlights the potential for a more integrative and patient-centered approach to healthcare.

CHAPTER 7
POLARITY THERAPY AND DAILY LIFE

The application of Polarity Therapy concepts to daily activities reflects a comprehensive approach to well-being, emphasizing the interdependence of mind, body, and spirit. Polarity Therapy is based on a knowledge of energy flow and balance, and it encourages people to incorporate its concepts into their daily lives.

This entails a conscious knowledge of the body's energetic dynamics, with a focus on the three basic energy centers: positive, negative, and neutral. Polarity Therapy practitioners advocate for mindfulness in actions, thoughts, and emotions, which aligns with the natural flow of energy.

This integration extends beyond formal therapeutic sessions to include daily activities like eating, exercising, and even talking. Individuals who incorporate Polarity concepts into their activities aim to maintain a harmonious energy flow, which promotes general well-being.

<u>Creating a Balanced Living Environment.</u>

The concept of creating a balanced living environment within the context of Polarity Therapy emphasizes the importance of external variables in influencing one's energetic stability.

According to Polarity Therapy, an individual's natural flow of energy can be supported or disrupted by their surroundings. A balanced living environment is achieved via the intentional design of physical spaces and the careful selection of components that encourage positive energy flow. This includes color palettes, lighting, and spatial configurations that are consistent with Polarity principles. Beyond the physical realm, the emotional and social aspects of the living environment are also important.

Establishing healthy connections, encouraging pleasant emotional experiences, and reducing stressors all contribute to a well-balanced living environment that supports Polarity Therapy principles. In essence, this notion promotes a holistic approach to well-being, emphasizing the interaction of internal and external forces.

<u>Polarity and Stress Management:</u>

Stress has become an integral component of modern life, affecting people physically, intellectually, and emotionally.

Polarity Therapy is a unique approach to stress management by treating the underlying causes within the body's energy framework.

This approach understands that stress disturbs the normal flow of energy, causing imbalances and, as a result, a variety of health disorders. Polarity in stress management refers to approaches and activities aimed at restoring and maintaining energy homeostasis.

These may include particular massage, breathwork, and mindful exercises designed to release blocked energy and relieve stress-related tension. Polarity Therapy, by addressing the energetic imbalances associated with stress, offers a complete approach that supplements traditional stress management treatments. Furthermore, it highlights the need for preventive measures, encouraging people to incorporate Polarity principles into their daily lives to develop resistance to stressors and promote long-term well-being.

Finally, Polarity Therapy is a holistic approach to well-being, with ideas that transcend beyond therapeutic sessions and influence many aspects of daily life.

Incorporating Polarity concepts into daily activities promotes a holistic approach, emphasizing the interdependence of mind, body, and spirit. Creating a healthy living environment necessitates deliberate design choices and attention, as well as an understanding of how external elements influence energy flow.

Furthermore, Polarity for stress management addresses the widespread issue of stress by recognizing and resolving energy imbalances, providing a holistic approach to restoring equilibrium and promoting long-term health. Polarity Therapy, using these notions, provides a framework for individuals to build a harmonic and energetically balanced life.

CHAPTER 8
CASE STUDIES AND SUCCESS STORIES

Polarity Therapy, a holistic approach to health and wellness, has gained attention and legitimacy via the use of case studies and success stories. These in-depth investigations of individual experiences provide vital insight into Polarity Therapy's efficacy and transformative potential. One appealing aspect of case studies is the examination of various health issues and the resulting outcomes achieved with this therapeutic approach. For example, researchers and practitioners have documented examples in which people with chronic pain, stress-related diseases, and even emotional imbalances had considerable increases in their general well-being after participating in Polarity Therapy sessions.

The use of real-life examples is critical in establishing Polarity Therapy's legitimacy and applicability across a wide range of health concerns. These case studies frequently go into the exact procedures used in Polarity Therapy sessions, giving insight into the complexities of energy balance, massage, and nutritional suggestions. Researchers and healthcare professionals can gain a deeper understanding of Polarity Therapy's complex approach to the connectivity of mind, body, and spirit by evaluating the course of a client's health journey.

Furthermore, success tales in the field of Polarity Therapy go beyond symptom relief; they capture the comprehensive aspect of the healing process. Clients frequently report not only physical gains, but also increased mental clarity, emotional resilience, and a stronger sense of spiritual wellbeing. These diverse outcomes highlight Polarity Therapy's complete character, which goes beyond the traditional confines of healthcare by adopting a holistic worldview that takes into account the interplay of numerous aspects influencing an individual's health.

As researchers investigate these cases, they discover patterns and connections that add to the expanding body of evidence supporting the efficacy of Polarity Therapy.

The documentation of successful interventions lays the groundwork for future research, encouraging rigorous scientific inquiry into the underlying mechanisms of action and the possibility of incorporating Polarity Therapy into conventional healthcare procedures.

<u>Client Experience and Transformations:</u>

Client experiences are the foundation of the Polarity Therapy story, providing personal descriptions of transformative journeys to improved health and well-being. These stories capture the profoundly personal and subjective aspect of the therapy process, offering insight into how Polarity Therapy may have a significant impact on people's lives. Clients frequently describe not only physical improvements but also shifts in their emotional and mental landscapes, providing a comprehensive view of the transforming impact of this therapeutic method.

The investigation of client experiences in the context of Polarity Therapy frequently begins with a study of the initial conditions and problems encountered by people seeking this type of holistic healing. Clients may present with a variety of difficulties, including medical diseases, emotional imbalances, and spiritual estrangement. Client narratives provide academics and practitioners with insights into the wide range of concerns that lead people to consider Polarity Therapy as a complementary approach to their general well-being.

One common thread in client stories is the emphasis on the therapeutic interaction between the practitioner and the client. Polarity Therapy sessions foster trust and rapport, creating a setting suitable for the discovery and release of energy blockages, supporting the individual's restoration of balance. Clients frequently experience a sense of empowerment and agency as they actively participate in the healing process, helping to co-create a harmonic and balanced state of being.

Furthermore, the transformative power of Polarity Therapy extends beyond the physical and emotional worlds to include the spiritual component of human existence. Clients commonly describe increased self-awareness, spiritual connection, and a new sense of purpose and vigor. These remarkable alterations highlight Polarity Therapy's holistic worldview, which sees individuals as interrelated beings rather than independent things.

The documentation of client transformations is also an important resource for the ongoing development and evolution of Polarity Therapy techniques.

Practitioners can modify and tailor their approaches to the different experiences shared by clients, resulting in a dynamic and responsive therapeutic framework. Furthermore, the collection of client narratives adds to the ongoing conversation between holistic practitioners and the broader healthcare community, fostering a better understanding of Polarity Therapy's potential benefits and applications within the larger context of integrative medicine.

Finally, investigating case studies and success stories in the field of Polarity Therapy yields a rich tapestry of data supporting its efficacy and transformative potential. Researchers and practitioners acquire significant insights into Polarity Therapy's various applications across a range of health issues by examining real-life instances and client narratives. The multiple effects reported by clients highlight the therapy modality's holistic nature, which addresses the interdependence of mind, body, and spirit. As the volume of evidence grows, the incorporation of Polarity Therapy into mainstream healthcare procedures becomes a topic of continuing investigation and debate, representing a viable route for the progress of holistic approaches to health and well-being.

CHAPTER 9
PROFESSIONAL PRACTICES AND ETHICS

Professional practice and ethics are critical in the field of Polarity Therapy, ensuring that practitioners follow a set of norms that prioritize their client's well-being and safety. Training and certification in Polarity Therapy are critical components of starting a professional practice. The training often includes a thorough understanding of the principles and procedures related to Polarity Therapy, such as energy anatomy, bodywork, and communication skills. The certification certifies a practitioner's ability to implement these techniques and guarantees a specific level of expertise in the subject.

The practice of Polarity Therapy requires ethical considerations to maintain the therapy's integrity and credibility. Practitioners must prioritize clients' autonomy and dignity while respecting their views, values, and boundaries. Informed consent is a key component of ethical practice, ensuring that clients understand the therapy process, potential risks, and benefits before starting with treatment. Another important consideration is confidentiality, which protects clients' privacy while still building a trusting therapy connection. Ethical rules include emphasizing cultural sensitivity, as well as the recognition and respect for client diversity.

Developing a successful Polarity Therapy practice requires a diverse approach that goes beyond clinical expertise. Practitioners must examine a variety of aspects, including marketing, client retention, and business management. Building a strong online and offline presence through efficient marketing methods is critical for attracting customers. Building a professional network and cooperating with other healthcare providers might help to grow the practice. Client retention entails offering quality services, cultivating positive therapeutic connections, and adjusting to the changing requirements of clients. Additionally, excellent business administration, such as financial planning and record-keeping, assures the long-term viability and success of a Polarity Therapy practice.

<u>Training and Certification for Polarity Therapy:</u>

Polarity Therapy training and certification serve as the foundation for the development of competent and skilled practitioners in the area. The training normally includes a thorough curriculum that covers Polarity Therapy's key principles, methodologies, and applications. This education frequently involves a thorough examination of the energetic anatomy, with a focus on the flow of energy through the body and its effects on physical, mental, and emotional well-being. Students also learn numerous bodywork techniques, communication skills, and ethical issues that are necessary for effective and responsible practice.

Hands-on experience and supervision are essential components of Polarity Therapy training. This enables students to apply theoretical information in a practical situation, improving their abilities and gaining a thorough understanding of how to interact with the body's energy system.

Supervised practice also allows students to receive comments and advice from experienced teachers, promoting the integration of theory and practice. Furthermore, training programs frequently include case studies, role-playing, and practical assessments to ensure that students are well-prepared for real-world situations.

Certification in Polarity Therapy is a professional accreditation that attests to a practitioner's competence and adherence to established industry standards. Certification is often awarded by respectable organizations or associations that promote and regulate Polarity Therapy. Written examinations, practical assessments, and demonstrations of ethical understanding may all be part of the certification process. This rigorous review assures that trained practitioners achieve the required levels of expertise and ethics, giving clients trust in Polarity Therapy treatments.

<u>Ethical Considerations for Practice:</u>

Polarity Therapy practitioners must prioritize ethical considerations, highlighting the need to maintain a high level of professionalism and honesty. Practitioners in this sector must follow a set of ethical norms that stress the well-being, autonomy, and dignity of their clients. Informed consent is a fundamental ethical concept that requires practitioners to present clients with detailed information about Polarity Therapy, its risks, and benefits before beginning any therapy.

This allows clients to make educated decisions about their participation in therapy.

Confidentiality is another important ethical consideration in Polarity Therapy. Practitioners must maintain client confidentiality while maintaining a trustworthy and secure therapy environment. This includes securing client records, verbal communications, and any other information exchanged throughout the therapeutic partnership. Respecting ethnic variety and recognizing the individuality of each client is also an ethical need. Practitioners must be culturally aware and empathetic, tailoring their approach to clients' different backgrounds and beliefs.

Boundary management is a difficult ethical issue in which practitioners must set and maintain proper professional boundaries with clients. This includes fostering a therapeutic connection that promotes the client's well-being while avoiding exploitation, manipulation, or parallel relationships. Clear communication and regular self-reflection are essential for managing these limits and keeping the therapy partnership focused on the client's needs.

Developing a Successful Polarity Therapy Practice:

Building a successful Polarity Therapy firm requires a deliberate and comprehensive strategy that includes components of business management, marketing, and client interaction. The development of clinical abilities through extensive Polarity Therapy training and certification is an essential component.

Practitioners must gain a thorough understanding of the principles and practices involved with Polarity Therapy to give successful and evidence-based therapies to their clients.

Effective marketing methods are critical for bringing clients into a Polarity Therapy practice. This entails creating a strong online presence via a professional website, social media platforms, and other digital means. Clear and informative content regarding the benefits of Polarity Therapy, the practitioner's qualifications, and the unique elements of their business can help to establish trust with potential clients. Networking within the healthcare community and cooperating with other practitioners can also help you gain awareness and referral prospects.

Client retention is an important aspect of the success of a Polarity Therapy practice. Client satisfaction and loyalty are enhanced by providing quality services, establishing strong therapeutic interactions, and exhibiting a commitment to clients' well-being. Practitioners must also stay current on developing trends in the area, always updating their abilities and customizing their practice to match the changing demands of their clientele. Seeking client input and accepting constructive criticism can help to improve service quality and the practitioner-client relationship.

Effective business management is essential for the longevity of a Polarity Therapy practice.

This includes financial planning, budgeting, and record-keeping to ensure the firm runs smoothly. Practitioners must also be aware of legal and regulatory obligations, and secure the relevant licenses or permissions. Implementing effective scheduling and administrative procedures can help the practice function more smoothly, allowing practitioners to focus on providing high-quality Polarity Therapy treatments to their customers.

CHAPTER 10
THE FUTURE OF POLARITY THERAPY

Polarity Therapy's future seems optimistic as it evolves and gains recognition in the field of complementary and alternative medicine. Dr. Randolph Stone developed this holistic approach to well-being, which combines Eastern and Western concepts to address the body's energetic flow. Advances in Polarity Therapy research are critical to guiding its future trajectory. Polarity Therapy's physiological and psychological effects are being investigated in research projects, to provide empirical data to back up its effectiveness. As technology and scientific methodology progress, researchers delve deeper into the subtle mechanics that underpin energy flow and the balancing strategies used in Polarity Therapy. Understanding the physiological foundation of energy imbalances and how Polarity Therapy interventions influence them helps to increase the practice's credibility and acceptance.

In addition to empirical research, emerging trends and technologies are propelling Polarity Therapy to new heights. Integrative techniques that incorporate Polarity Therapy with other complementary therapies, such as acupuncture or massage therapy, are becoming increasingly popular.

These synergistic approaches offer a more holistic approach to health and wellness. Furthermore, technology improvements are enabling remote Polarity Therapy sessions, allowing practitioners to reach a larger audience and providing convenient access to people in various geographical regions.

The use of virtual and augmented reality technologies may improve the therapeutic experience by providing immersive environments that maximize the effects of Polarity Therapy.

Global viewpoints on Polarity Therapy have a huge impact on its future growth. As the world becomes more interconnected, Polarity Therapy's numerous cultural interpretations and applications improve its practice. Cross-cultural cooperation allows for the exchange of knowledge and experiences, which promotes a more inclusive and adaptive approach to energy healing. Polarity Therapy is being integrated into mainstream healthcare systems around the world, which is also a major trend. Recognition by healthcare professionals and institutions supports Polarity Therapy's efficacy, establishing it as a reputable and sustainable supplementary technique. Polarity Therapy's future depends not just on its continuing evolution, but also on its integration into varied cultural and healthcare contexts around the world.

Advancements in Polarity Therapy Research

Advances in Polarity Therapy research are helping to understand the mechanics and benefits of this comprehensive approach to health and well-being. Researchers are increasingly using rigorous scientific methods to study the physiological, psychological, and energy components of Polarity Therapy. One important field of research is understanding the energy pathways in the body and how disruptions in these pathways relate to physical and mental health problems. Advanced imaging tools, such as functional magnetic resonance imaging (fMRI) and bioelectromagnetic measures, provide light on the tiny energy changes that occur during Polarity Therapy sessions.

Furthermore, Polarity Therapy is being studied for its effects on the autonomic nervous system, endocrine system, and immunological response. Polarity Therapy interventions have been proven in studies to impact the sympathetic and parasympathetic nervous systems' balance, increasing relaxation and lowering stress. Polarity Therapy's effects on hormone control and immune function are also being studied, which will shed light on how it can benefit general health and resilience. These scientific investigations are critical for developing a robust evidence base that can be incorporated into standard healthcare practices.

In addition to physiological studies, there is growing interest in the psychological elements of Polarity Therapy. Researchers are looking at how Polarity Therapy interventions affect mood, cognitive performance, and emotional well-being. Psychometric tests and qualitative research methodologies are used to capture individuals' subjective experiences during Polarity Therapy. Understanding the psychological factors at work improves our understanding of how this comprehensive strategy might benefit mental health and emotional balance.

As research approaches evolve, there will likely be an increase in randomized controlled trials, systematic reviews, and meta-analyses investigating the efficacy of Polarity Therapy for specific health issues. The use of objective measurements, such as biomarkers and physiological indicators, in research designs improves the scientific rigor of studies investigating the effects of Polarity Therapy. Finally, developments in research are critical to establishing Polarity Therapy as a reputable and evidence-based supplementary treatment in the larger healthcare environment.

Emerging Trends and Innovation

Polarity Therapy is seeing a surge of new trends and innovations that are altering its methods and broadening its scope. One significant trend is the combination of Polarity

Therapy with various alternative treatments, resulting in a more comprehensive and synergistic approach to overall wellness. Collaborations with therapies such as acupuncture, massage therapy, and mindfulness techniques improve the total therapeutic experience by addressing not just energetic imbalances, but also physical and emotional health. This integrative approach is consistent with the holistic idea of Polarity Therapy and provides patients with a diverse toolkit for improving their health.

Technological advances are also influencing the future of Polarity Therapy. The development of virtual and augmented reality applications for energy therapy is gaining popularity. These technologies provide immersive surroundings that enhance the benefits of Polarity Therapy, resulting in a multisensory experience for those attending sessions. Remote Polarity Therapy sessions are now possible thanks to virtual platforms, making the treatment more accessible to people who do not live near a certified practitioner. As technology advances, these technologies have the potential to transform the delivery and accessibility of Polarity Therapy services.

Another developing trend is the integration of Polarity Therapy into corporate wellness initiatives and healthcare settings. Employers are recognizing the need for holistic approaches to employee well-being, and Polarity Therapy is finding its way into workplace wellness efforts. Furthermore, healthcare organizations are looking into incorporating Polarity Therapy alongside traditional medical treatments, recognizing its potential for meeting patients' holistic requirements. These trends point to a more integrative and inclusive approach to health, with Polarity Therapy playing an important role in creating balance and harmony on numerous levels.

Furthermore, the global use of Polarity Therapy promotes cross-cultural exchange and adaptation. Polarity Therapy is viewed and applied differently depending on cultural beliefs and energy healing traditions. This diversity enhances the profession, enabling a more inclusive and adaptable approach to holistic well-being. As Polarity Therapy evolves, new trends and innovations strengthen its resilience and relevance in a quickly changing healthcare context.

Global Perspectives on Polarity Therapy.

The global perspectives on Polarity Therapy emphasize the various cultural interpretations and applications of this comprehensive approach to health and well-being. As Polarity Therapy crosses cultural barriers, it is adapted and integrated into diverse therapeutic traditions around the world. Cross-cultural viewpoints add to the depth of Polarity Therapy techniques by reflecting universal principles of energy balance while recognizing cultural differences and variety.

Polarity Therapy resonates with Eastern cultures, where ancient practices such as acupuncture and Ayurveda have long been entrenched. The combination of Polarity Therapy and these historic traditions strengthens the holistic framework, providing a synergistic approach to balancing energy and enhancing general health. Polarity

Therapy is gaining popularity as a complement to conventional treatment in Western societies. Healthcare practitioners and institutions are recognizing its importance in addressing the energetic components of health, as well as its ability to improve the whole therapy experience.

Cultural variety also influences the approaches and modalities used during Polarity Therapy sessions. Practitioners may be inspired by traditional healing methods, combining aspects like as breathwork, meditation, and bodywork techniques unique to their cultural backgrounds. This versatility guarantees that Polarity Therapy remains relevant and accessible to people from all cultural backgrounds, building a global community of practitioners and recipients.

Furthermore, cross-cultural cooperation promotes the sharing of knowledge and experiences in the field of energy therapy. International conferences, workshops, and training programs provide opportunities for practitioners from around the world to share insights and improve their abilities.

This collaborative approach not only broadens our understanding of Polarity Therapy but also helps to build standardized methods that may be applied in a variety of cultural and healthcare situations.

As Polarity Therapy gains global recognition, its integration into mainstream healthcare systems is becoming a reality in many areas. Polarity Therapy's recognition by regulatory organizations and healthcare institutions supports it as a genuine and effective supplementary technique. This universal recognition establishes Polarity Therapy as a vital resource for people seeking holistic approaches to health and well-being, regardless of cultural origin.

CONCLUSION

Polarity Therapy's future is defined by improvements in research, rising trends and innovations, and global perspectives, all of which contribute to its evolution and incorporation into mainstream healthcare. Scientific research into its physiological and psychological impacts strengthens its legitimacy, while trends such as integrative approaches and technological advancements increase its reach and impact. Polarity Therapy's worldwide viewpoints reflect its versatility across various cultural traditions, promoting a more inclusive and enriched approach to overall well-being. As Polarity Therapy develops, its potential to contribute to the worldwide landscape of complementary and alternative medicine grows, offering a future in which energy healing is accepted as an intrinsic part of holistic healthcare practices.